Amazing Nature

perfect Partners

John Woodward

Heinemann Library
Chicago, Illinois

Produced for Heinemann Library by Discovery Books Limited
Originated by Ambassador Litho Ltd
Printed in China by South China Printing Company

08 07 06 05 04
10 9 8 7 6 5 4 3 2 1

Library of Congress Cataloging-in-Publication Data
Woodward, John, 1954-
  Perfect partners / John Woodward.
      p. cm. -- (Amazing nature)
Summary: Describes various examples of symbiosis, the elaborate give-and-take of food, shelter, and other essentials of life that goes on between different kinds of animals and plants.
Includes bibliographical references (p.   ) and index.
  ISBN 1-4034-4708-X (hardcover) -- ISBN 1-4034-5404-3 (pbk.)
  1. Symbiosis--Juvenile literature. [1. Symbiosis.] I. Title. II. Series.
  QH548.W66 2003
  577.8'5--dc22
                              2003022044

Acknowledgments
The publisher would like to thank the following for permission to reproduce photographs:
p. 4 Yves Lanceau/Natural History Photographic Agency; p. 5 Roger Tidman/Natural History Photographic Agency; p. 6A Nigel J. Dennis/Natural History Photographic Agency; p. 6B Anthony Bannister/Natural History Photographic Agency; p. 7 Roger Hosking/FLPA: p. 8 Nigel J. Dennis/Natural History Photographic Agency; pp. 9, 10 Minden Pictures/FLPA: p. 11 Carl Roessler/Oxford Scientific Films; p. 12 Colin Marshall/FLPA; p. 13 Max Gibbs/Oxford Scientific Films; p. 14 Partridge Films Ltd./Oxford Scientific Films; p. 15 Dr. Ivan Polunin/Natural History Photographic Agency; p. 16 Kim Taylor/Bruce Coleman Collection; p. 17 N. A. Callow/Natural History Photographic Agency; p. 18 Minden Pictures/FLPA; p. 19A Andrew Purcell/Bruce Coleman Collection; p. 19B Staffan Widstrand/Bruce Coleman Collection; p. 20 Photodisc; p. 21 Gerard Lacz/FLPA; p. 22 Eric Soder/Natural History Photographic Agency; p. 23 Anthony Bannister/Natural History Photographic Agency; p. 24 Ken Preston-Mafham/Premaphotos Wildlife; p. 25 Ken Preston-Mafham/Premaphotos Wildlife; p. 26 Partridge Films Ltd/Oxford Scientific Films; p. 27 John Hawkins/FLPA; p. 28 P. Kaya/Bruce Coleman Collection; p. 29 Christophe Ratier/Natural History Photographic Agency.

Cover photograph of a western clown anemonefish on a sea anemone: B. Jones & M. Shimlock/Natural History Photographic Agency.

Every effort has been made to contact copyright holders of any material reproduced in this book. Any omissions will be rectified in subsequent printings if notice is given to the publisher.

Some words are shown in bold, **like this.** You can find out what they mean by looking in the glossary.

Contents

Living Together 4

Smart Birds .6

Pest Pickers .8

Service Station 10

Poisonous Protection 12

Defending Armies 14

Aphid Farm 16

The Power of Sunlight 18

Food Processors 20

Fungus Gardeners 22

Sweet Temptation 24

Planting Service 26

Fact File 28

Glossary 30

More Books to Read 31

Index 32

Living Together

Life is tough, but it gets easier if you have a little help from your friends. Living together is often safer than living alone. Animals that live together can help each other find food, make homes, and stay warm in winter.

Usually the animals that live together belong to the same **species,** but sometimes two or more very different species share their lives. One species may steal something from the other one, and give nothing back. That makes it a **parasite**. Other species are real partners, and each species helps the other. This kind of arrangement is called **symbiosis** (sim-bye-oh-sis).

The sea anemones clinging to this hermit crab get extra food from whatever the crab catches and leaves. In return, they defend the crab from its enemies with their painful stings.

Small birds like these greenfinches and bramblings often team up to look for food in winter, but they live apart in summer.

Short and long partnerships

Many symbiotic partnerships do not last long. Different species come together, take whatever they need from each other, then split up. The mixed flocks of small birds that search for food together in winter are like this. They help each other watch out for danger as they feed, so staying in a flock makes good sense. But for the rest of the year, they can manage quite well on their own.

Other species form symbiotic partnerships for life. They never split up, and if they did, they would soon be in deep trouble. For example, many animals cannot **digest** their food without the help of tiny **microbes** that live in their stomachs, and the microbes can live nowhere else. These partners must stay together to survive.

Smart Birds

Some birds have learned to team up with other animals to find food. One of the best examples of such birds is the black-throated honeyguide, which lives in African forests. The honeyguide eats the waxy honeycombs made by wild bees. As the honeyguide is not strong enough to break into the bees' nests itself, it gets help.

Its favorite partner is an African honey badger. The badger has strong teeth and claws, and it loves honey. The honeyguide dances in front of it, making a chattering call, then flies off a little way. The badger understands this is a sign, and follows. The honeyguide keeps leading the badger until they get to the nest. Then the badger breaks into the nest and enjoys a feast of honey while the bird eats the honeycomb.

This honey badger will have no trouble breaking into a wild bees' nest, but it needs a honeyguide (above) to show it where to find one.

Bird and human partnerships

Honeyguides also lead humans to bees' nests. Africans have used them, just like the honey badger does, for thousands of years. Another long-lasting partnership between birds and humans features the barn owl, which hunts small **mammals** over grassland. When humans began to cut down trees to create farmland, barn owls had many more places to hunt. The owls also discovered that farm buildings such as barns made ideal places to nest. Traditional farmers still use barns for storing the grain they harvest from their crops. They want barn owls to nest in their barns because the owls catch and eat lots of rats and mice that would otherwise eat the grain.

The barn owl nests in a barn and repays the farmer by catching rats and mice to feed her fluffy chicks.

Pest Pickers

Many big **mammals** that feed on the grasslands of Africa are attacked by tiny creatures, such as flies, that suck their blood or burrow into their flesh. Since the big animals have hooves rather than claws or fingernails, they cannot easily scratch these **parasites** off their skin. Birds called oxpeckers come to their rescue. They have very strong, sharp claws on their feet that grip the thick skin of animals like rhinoceroses, giraffes, and buffaloes. Oxpeckers are experts at finding pests on these animals, picking them off with their bright red or yellow beaks, and eating them.

A red-billed oxpecker can get at the parts that an impala cannot reach, and earn itself a tasty snack in the process.

Tortoises and finches

On the Galapagos Islands in the Pacific Ocean off South America, giant tortoises enjoy the same attention. Small birds called finches hop over their skin, picking off the parasites that the tortoises cannot reach. The tortoises show they want to be groomed by raising their heavy bodies off the ground. This allows the birds to reach into every wrinkle in the tortoises' leathery skin.

This giant tortoise has no way of removing bloodsucking ticks from its skin, so it gets a little finch to do the job.

Another bird behaves in the same way as the Galapagos finches but in a very different place. Out at sea, a bird called the red phalarope picks parasites off the skin of whales. The whales rise to the ocean surface and allow the birds to poke about and rip away bloodsucking pests.

Service Station

You might be surprised to learn that fish are targeted by bloodsucking **parasites** just as badly as land animals are. Some of the worst pests attach themselves to the fishes' gills, which are rows of delicate, blood-filled tubes that take in oxygen from the water. The walls of these tubes are very thin, so small bloodsuckers find them easy to attack.

On **coral reefs,** small, banded shrimp pick pests from the skin and gills of fish. These cleaner shrimp gather at special sites on the reef and the big fish line up, patiently waiting their turn to be picked over by the shrimps' nimble **pincers.**

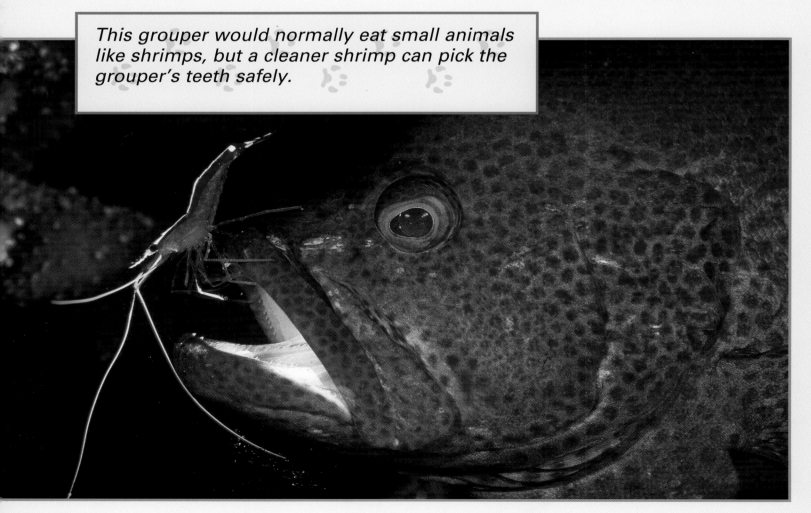

This grouper would normally eat small animals like shrimps, but a cleaner shrimp can pick the grouper's teeth safely.

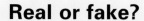

Real or fake?

Some small, striped fish called cleaner wrasses do the same job. They dart all over their customers, in and out of their gills, and even enter their mouths, picking off parasites and food remains with their teeth. Many of the big fish are fierce hunters, yet they never eat the small cleaners. They recognize them, partly by their behavior, and partly by their stripes.

Nibbling away harmful skin parasites gives the cleaner wrasse a meal and keeps the bigger fish healthy.

Yet some of the cleaners are fakes. One small fish, a blenny called *Aspidontus*, is striped like a cleaner wrasse and pretends to be just as useful. But when a big fish lets it get close enough, the blenny darts in and takes a bite out of it!

11

Poisonous Protection

Corals and sea anemones are armed with thousands of tiny stingers that work like poisonous darts. They use them to catch their **prey,** but these stingers also make very good weapons to defend the corals and anemones against big fish and other enemies.

Some small fish called clown fish are not harmed by these stings. Clown fish hide among the stinging **tentacles** of big **tropical** sea anemones. The stingers protect the clown fish from bigger fish, just as they protect the anemone, but it is not obvious what the anemone gets out of the arrangement. It is possible that the anemone simply does not mind having a lodger.

Every one of these soft sea anemone tentacles is armed with hundreds of stingers, but they have no effect on the little clown fish.

*This **coral reef** boxer crab has a powerful punch, thanks to the stinging sea anemones that it wears on its pincers like gloves.*

Weapons for a crab

The hermit crabs that live in the empty shells of sea snails sometimes carry sea anemones around with them. This is often accidental, but one **species** does it on purpose. The anemone completely covers the crab's shell like a stinging quilt. It protects the crab from its enemies in return for scraps of food. When the crab grows too big for its borrowed shell, it moves into a bigger one. The anemone moves too, with a little help from the crab.

Another species of crab attaches an anemone to each of its **pincers**. It uses them like a pair of stinging boxing gloves, to fight off its enemies. The anemones don't mind being used like this because they pick up plenty of food as the crab feeds.

Defending Armies

Many insects are armed with stingers and biting jaws, which they use to defend their nests. Some of the fiercest defenders are ants, and some plants use ants to protect them from plant-eating animals.

One of the most amazing is the bulls horn acacia, which lives in Central America. It grows fat thorns that are especially attractive to ants. The ants hollow them out and use them as nests. The acacia also supplies the ants with a sugary food, which they love, and a special extra-rich food that is ideal for young ants.

Hungry acacia ants drink sugary **nectar** supplied by the acacia tree in return for their services as a defending army.

The ants, however, need more food than the acacia plant offers, so they also attack any insects that land on the plant. Many of these insects are leaf eaters that could strip all the leaves from the acacia, so the ants do the plant a favor by killing its enemies. They are like a defending army.

Eating the leftovers

Another tropical plant uses ants in a different way. The ant plant lives in **mangrove** swamps. It grows high up on the branch of a mangrove tree so it cannot get its food from the ground. Instead, it has a wide, hollow stem that provides a home for ants. The ants bring their insect **prey** back to the nest and dump the leftovers in special chambers. There, the waste rots and supplies the plant with all the food it needs.

The strange ant plant gets ants to keep it supplied with food, while the ants use the hollow stems of the plant as nests.

15

Aphid Farm

Many plants are attacked by aphids, small bugs that feed on plants' sugary **sap**. The aphids need to eat a lot of sap to get the **protein** they need to grow and produce young. They use some of it but get rid of the rest as a sweet syrup called honeydew.

Ants love honeydew. Whenever they find a swarm of feeding aphids they gather the honeydew from the aphids' bodies. But the ants do more than that. They treat the aphids rather like dairy cows, and milk them of honeydew in exchange for protecting the aphids from their enemies. These enemies include ladybugs and their **larvae,** and the larvae of lacewing flies and hoverflies.

These big wood ants are gathering sweet honeydew from small, dark aphids feeding on sugary sap high in a birch tree.

Garden ants even look after aphids' eggs during the winter, so they can start new colonies in spring. If the ants end up with too many aphids, they just eat them!

Aphid shelters

The ants usually keep these killers away by staying near the aphids. But some ants use earth and plant material to build aphid shelters at the base of plant stems. The entrances to the shelters are too small for the hunters to enter, and the ants often pick up the aphids and carry them into the shelters for protection.

Black garden ants may even carry aphids into their underground nests. They place the aphids in special chambers. There the aphids feed on the sap in growing plant roots.

The Power of Sunlight

Some animals are partners with tiny **algae** that are too small to see without a microscope. These algae are able to use the energy of sunlight to make sugar out of air and water. This process is called **photosynthesis** (foh-toh-sin-thuh-sis), and it is also used by all green plants. No animal can make food in this way, but if it teams up with the right algae it can take some of the sugars that the algae produce. In exchange, it gives the algae food and somewhere to live.

The most famous of these animals are corals. A coral is a simple animal that gathers food from the water with stinging **tentacles.** Its body also contains thousands of food-making algae. The corals that form **tropical coral reefs** get most of their food from their algae, so they grow only in clear, shallow water where there is plenty of sunlight to power their tiny sugar factories.

A coral reef is like an underwater garden, growing in the tropical sunshine that gleams through the crystal-clear water.

The giant clams that live on coral reefs use the same trick. The thick, fleshy lips lining their shells are brightly colored by the food-making algae that live there. Like coral, a giant clam can gather bits of food from the water. But clear, tropical seas do not have a lot of food floating in them, so the clam relies on its partnership with algae to keep it alive.

The soft lips of a giant clam are home to thousands of tiny algae, which repay the clam with sugar that they make using the energy of sunlight.

Lichen and coral links

The strange, plant-like lichens that grow on rocks and walls use algae in the same way as corals do. A lichen is actually a mixture of a **fungus** and a mass of colorful algae.

A partnership between a fungus and plant-like algae allows this lichen to live on a bare rock, where neither could survive alone.

Food Processors

Many **mammals** such as deer, giraffes, sheep, and horses eat leaves or grass. Such foods are easy to find, but they are not ideal. Leaves contain a lot of tough material called **cellulose**. Most plant-eating animals cannot turn it into useful food.

These animals get help from tiny **microbes** that live in their stomachs. Most of these microbes are particular types of **bacteria** that can live in dark, airless places. The bacteria can break down the cellulose and turn it into sugar. They use this sugar as food for themselves, but they also produce other substances that their mammal partner can use as food. Eventually, the bacteria themselves are **digested**.

Giraffes rely on the microbes in their stomachs to digest the leaves of acacia trees. Without the microbes, the giraffes would starve.

Designed for grazing

All this digestion takes time, so mammals that eat leaves or grass have big stomachs and very long **intestines** to allow the bacteria time to do their job properly. Many also have very complicated digestive systems, with different chambers that do different jobs.

These leaf- and grass-eating mammals need to get their bacteria from somewhere. The young koala, which feeds on the leaves of eucalyptus trees in Australian forests, gets its bacteria from its mother. When the young koala is ready to eat leaves, its mother squirts some half-digested eucalyptus out of her back end. The baby eats it, and the bacteria then start multiplying inside its own stomach.

This baby koala is getting its first taste of eucalyptus leaves. The leaves are poisonous to most animals, but adult koalas never eat anything else.

Fungus Gardeners

The leaf cutter ants that live in Central and South America are famous for the way they slice up leaves and carry the pieces back to their giant underground nests. When they get the leaves home they chew them up, but they don't actually eat them. The ants cannot **digest** leaves properly because they do not have helpful bacteria in their stomachs to do the job. Instead, they have help in a different form.

The ants feed the chewed leaves to a type of **fungus** that lives only in their nests. Unlike the ants, the fungus can turn the leaves into useful food, so it grows well. The ants look after the fungus carefully, like tiny gardeners. They keep it aired and watered, and get rid of any pests that might attack it. Then, they eat it.

This leaf cutter ant does not eat the leaf pieces that it carries back to its nest. It feeds them to a fungus, and later eats the fungus.

The ants do not eat all of the fungus. As it grows, the fungus produces swellings on its stems. The ants harvest these, rather like picking apples from a tree. These lumps make good food, and the ants never need anything else. They just need to keep the fungus supplied with pieces of chewed leaf.

The special fungus being eaten by this baby termite can grow only inside termites' nests. The fungus needs the termites as much as the termites need the fungus.

Some termites also do this. Termites are kind of like ants, and they, too, live in huge nests. Many termites are able to make a meal of almost anything, including wooden houses, but some cannot digest **cellulose**. They solve the problem by making fungus gardens inside their nests, just like leaf cutter ants.

Sweet Temptation

Flowers are very tempting to insects and birds because they contain **nectar,** a sweet food that contains lots of energy. As they feed, the animals get covered in the flowers' powdery **pollen.** They then carry the pollen to other flowers, where it brushes off and **fertilizes** them. For this to work well, the animal has to fly straight to another plant of the same **species.** If it goes to a different type of plant, the pollen is wasted. So some plants have found ways of making animals ignore other types of flowers, and only feed from theirs.

When a bumblebee lands on a snapdragon flower, its weight opens the blossom so it can get at the nectar. Other types of insect are not heavy enough, so the bumblebee prefers to feed from snapdragons because they are more likely to contain nectar. As it moves, it carries pollen from one snapdragon to another.

The weight of this fat bumblebee opens the snapdragon, allowing it to get at the sweet nectar. It repays the plant by carrying its pollen from snapdragon to snapdragon.

Long tongues and bills

Some plants have small flowers with petals that form long tubes. Only insects with very long tongues, such as butterflies, can reach their nectar.

Long-tongued butterflies prefer tubular flowers, because they are more likely to contain nectar than broad, open flowers that other animals can reach into.

In **tropical** South and Central America, large, tubular flowers attract long-billed hummingbirds in this way. For example, the nectar of daturas can be reached only by the amazing sword-billed hummingbird, whose bill is as long as the rest of its body! The datura and the hummingbird are perfect partners, since each gets exactly what it wants.

Planting Service

Some plants have animal partners that spread their seeds. In **tropical** forests, many trees produce seeds that are hidden inside sweet, juicy fruits. The fruits attract hungry animals such as birds, monkeys, and fruit bats, which eat the soft fruits and the seeds inside them. Then they move around the forest with the seeds in their stomachs. The tough seeds pass straight through their **intestines** without being harmed. Eventually the seeds are dumped far away from their parent tree, along with a lump of manure to help them grow.

Acacia seeds eaten by African elephants pass through their stomachs undigested. Tiny acacia trees eventually sprout from piles of elephant dung.

Many plants that grow in the tops of forest trees are planted like this. The mistletoe plants that grow in Australian forests even have a full-time partner called the mistletoe bird. The bird eats the sticky mistletoe berries, and when they emerge at its other end they are still sticky. The bird has to wipe its hind parts against rough tree bark to get rid of them, and this wedges the seeds in the places where they will grow.

European oak trees rely on jays to carry their seeds away and bury them, and then forget where they are.

European oak trees are partners with birds called jays. The jays love eating acorns, which are the tree's seeds. As winter approaches the jays bury huge numbers of acorns to eat later, when food becomes difficult to find. A lot of the acorns are never dug up, so they sprout and become young oak trees.

Fact File

Coral can survive only in shallow, sunlit water. This is because their **algae** need the light to make food. If the sea level rises, coral grows upward to stay near the surface. Some coral reefs have been growing upward for 50 million years, and are over 3,281 feet (1,000 meters) thick.

The underground nests of leaf cutter ants can be huge, with enough room for a grown person to stand up inside. Sometimes old nests built beneath forest roads cave in beneath the weight of a truck, and the truck disappears into the hole.

Ants probably have more strange relationships with other animals than any other group of creatures. Some form partnerships with butterfly caterpillars, carrying them into their nests. These caterpillars eat some of the ant **larvae** in the nest, but since they also supply the ants with sweet juices the ants do not seem to mind.

Scientists think that nearly all big animals have **microbes** in their stomachs that help them **digest** their food. Humans also have them. Some of these microbes are able to turn **cellulose** into sugar using a special substance which most animals cannot produce themselves. But slugs and snails can, and this allows them to digest tough plants with no trouble at all. That is why they are such pests in the garden!

The **fungus** gardens inside the nests of termites produce heat as they grow. So the termites build their nests with special air conditioning systems to keep them from overheating. The air conditioning works so well that the temperature inside the nest always stays the same, at almost exactly 86 °F (30 °C).

Glossary

algae   tiny, plant-like living things that can make food using the energy of sunlight

bacteria   tiny living things that multiply by splitting in two. Some cause diseases, while we need others to survive.

cellulose   tough fiber that gives plants their strength

coral reef   colony made up of thousands of tiny animals that build a hard skeleton around their soft bodies. They share food. Coral lives in shallow, sunlit seas, where their skeletons form reefs.

digest   to break down food into useful substances

fertilize   to make a seed or an egg fertile, so it grows into a plant or animal

fungus   type of living thing that looks like a plant, but feeds more like an animal

intestine   long, coiled tube leading from an animal's stomach, where its food is digested

larva (more than one are called larvae)   young form of an insect that does not look like its parents

mammal   warm-blooded, furry animal that feeds its young on milk produced by the mother

mangrove   type of tropical tree that grows in mud and water, often near the mouth of a river

microbe   very small living thing that cannot be seen without using a microscope

nectar   sweet, fragrant fluid produced by flowers and eaten by insects and birds

parasite   living thing that feeds on other living things while they are still alive

photosynthesis   process of making sugar out of carbon dioxide (from the air) and water, using the energy of sunlight

pincer   snapping claw of shrimp, lobsters, and crabs

pollen   fine dust produced by flowers that fertilizes other flowers

prey   animal that is attacked and eaten by another animal

protein   substance made by a living thing to build its body and often used as food by animals

sap   fluid that carries sugar and other substances around plants

species   particular type of animal

symbiosis   two living things in a partnership that benefits them both

tentacle   long, flexible, sensitive arm found on sea anemones, coral, and similar animals

tropical   describes hot regions of the world where the sun is directly overhead for part of the year

More Books to Read

Bailey, Jill. *How Insects Work Together.* Tarrytown, N.Y.: Marshall Cavendish, 1998.

Fredericks, Anthony D. and Sneed B. Collard. *Amazing Animals: Nature's Most Incredible Creatures.* Chanhassen, Minn.: Creative Publishing International, 2000.

Kalman, Bobbie. *What Are Food Chains and Webs?* New York: Crabtree Publishing, 1998.

Index

algae 18–19, 28
ant plants 15
ants 14–15, 16–17, 22–23, 28
aphids 16–17

bacteria 20–21, 22
barn owls 7
black-throated honeyguides 6–7
blennies 11
boxer crabs 13
bramblings 5
bulls horn acacia 14–15
bumblebees 24
butterflies 25, 28

cleaner shrimp 10
cleaner wrasses 11
clown fish 12
corals 10, 12, 18–19, 28

daturas 25
digestion 5, 20–21, 22–23, 26, 29

elephants 26

flowers 24–25
fruit bats 26
fungi 19, 22–23, 29

Galapagos finches 9
giant clams 19
giant tortoises 9
giraffes 8, 20

greenfinches 5
groupers 10

hermit crabs 4, 13
honey badgers 6
hummingbirds 25

impalas 8

jays 27

koalas 21

lichens 19

microbes 5, 20–21, 29
mistletoe birds 27
mistletoe plants 27
monkeys 26

oaks 27
oxpeckers 8

parasites 4, 8–9, 10–11
photosynthesis 18

red phalaropes 9

sea anemones 4, 12, 13
slugs 29
snails 13, 29
snapdragons 24

termites 23, 29

whales 9